Esther O'Gallagher's Lawrence Ashley Memories

ESTHER O'GALLAGHER

WESTBOW
PRESS®
A DIVISION OF THOMAS NELSON
& ZONDERVAN

WestBow Press books may be ordered through booksellers or by contacting:

WestBow Press
A Division of Thomas Nelson & Zondervan
1663 Liberty Drive
Bloomington, IN 47403
www.westbowpress.com
1 (866) 928-1240

ISBN: 978-1-5127-2281-9 (sc)
ISBN: 978-1-5127-2280-2 (e)

Library of Congress Control Number: 2015920242

Print information available on the last page.

WestBow Press rev. date: 2/3/2016

Acknowledgements

"The Rise and Fall of the Great Powers" Paul Kennedy
For the assistance with graphs and historical data.
Lawrence Ashley and Family who support is essential.
The Patriots King James Version

Disclaimer

This book is a tribute to the life of Lawrence Ashley CPA, student of economics, a believer in our Lord & Savior Jesus Christ, parent, carpenter, who researched, studied economics. The knowledge, documentation he sought to contribute to make a difference in society. These facts are a tribute to his research and knowledge.

Lawrence Ashley loved the Lord with all his heart, and dedicated his life to helping others. He is survived by his loving wife Mary Ashley the parent of Westley and Vanessa Ashley and a leader in the community. This book is a tribute to his life, knowledge and accomplishments through the Lord Jesus Christ who gives knowledge and wisdom to all.

I wish also to thank Victor Mordecai for his knowledge, providing vital insight to several chapters in this book. I am very grateful for his experience and knowledge.

Chapter

One

My View as an

Economic Student

In my research, I read an article by an economist who said that either there were some gross errors in current economic theory or the nature of the economy had somehow drastically changed from what it was thirty or forty years ago. He said that the economy now is often operating exactly the opposite of what is called for under current economic theory. He said that what was needed was some theory changes as dramatically different from the current economic theory as the Aggregate Demand and Aggregate Supply changes of John Maynard Keynes were different from Classical Economics.

In 1968 I took a course on economics in college, the first idea of what to expect were perhaps faulty, we generally think expect to experience some logic statements and probability theories and what experience the student brings to class is faulty because economics is just not everybody's favorite course.

Economics starts with a basic principle which everyone takes under assumption that this hypothesis is true but it may not have been proven or even checked out just carried from year to year.

Economic books are filled with data, charts, graphs and mathematical formulas. Many students expect basically all economics consist of is studying enough jargons terms to repeat the data back on exams.

The students figure that all they will be able to do is recognize when politicians seem to be using the right terms and theories, they don't really think they can ever understand economics.

In my experience, it never dawns on the students that they should actually look at the data themselves to check out the accuracy of what they are learning. If they took the time to analyze the data themselves they would learn much of what they are being taught is absolutely false.

Students are taught that a general principle of economics is that the level of spending determines the level of production and employment. This is what is known as demand side of economics. It then follows that all the government has to do is make sure enough spending takes place to fully employ everyone and to have the economy operate at full employment.

Students are taught about the multiplier effect which allows for the production increase to be greater than the spending increase. The idea is that we can precisely determine the effect of any given change in spending.

The obvious fact never seems to be realized that for there to be an increase in spending there will be also an increase in production and employment. The increase in employment and production leads to a real increase in spending this would be the correct way to perceive this fact.

The causative factors on the supply side, just as there are causative factors on the demand side. The changes in real production cause real changes in spending.

But not all changes in spending cause are real changes in spending and they do not cause real changes in production and employment.

Furthermore, not all changes in spending which cause changes in production continue to do that. These changes in spending shortly disappear into price changes instead and have only produced temporary surges in production which quickly reverse themselves.

In fact, in the long-run it is only supply side of economics which gives any real lasting changes in the economy. Modern economics, however, hardly admits the existence. The existence of any supply side causes and deals almost exclusively with demand side economics.

Students are taught a theory of price behavior which was first put forward by John Maynard Keynes in his book "The General Theory of Employment, Interest and Money in 1935." The price theory says that if the economy has high unemployment and less than optimum production, an increase in the level of spending can be fully absorbed in increasing production and employment without changing prices.

This is supposedly so because goods and services can be bought at the going price under these circumstances. People are willing to go to work at the going price. People are willing to sell more goods at the going price.

Therefore, an increase in spending can be used to call forth additional production and employment without changing prices. Furthermore it is taught that that this increased level of spending continues to be absorbed by production and employment rather than in general price level changes.

It is admitted that since everything does not adjust perfectly that there is some premature inflation.

The idea is that until we reach near full employment of people and resources there is near perfect absorption of money supply increases in production and employment increases with little or no changes in general price levels.

However, once we near full employment or reach full employment called the point of inelasticity of aggregate supply then increases in spending or the money supply represent excess demand which can only cause pure inflation since the resources cannot be employed more than 100%.

If we were to draw a graph whereby prices remain relatively flat as spending increases until near full employment at which point prices increase in direct proportion to the increase in the money supply.

Inflation caused by increasing the level of spending faster than the level of production can go up is called demand pull inflation. This is considered by economists to be the primary cause of inflation. If businesses or people have more control than they should in the economy and can cause their prices to increase in an unwarranted fashion before full employment is reached it is called cost-push inflation.

The Keynesian price theory that points at below full production spending increases result in production changes rather than general price level changes and therefore there should be little or no connection between the changes in the money supply and the change in the general price level or the level of production.

The employment flies directly in the face of the previously held price theory known as the quantity of money theory of prices. The Keynesian price theory differs from the Quantity of money price theory, but the entire truth of the Keynesian theory hangs on the truth of the Keynesian Price theory. If the price theory is untrue the entire Keynesian-demand side theory is false.

The quantity of money theory of prices said that prices tend to move in direct proportion to changes in the money supply. There had been considerable evidence to support the quantity theory over close to four hundred years up until 1933.

The importation of gold and silver from the new world into Europe led to continuous inflation that directly followed the distribution of that gold and silver into the currencies of Europe and basically in proportion to the increase in the money supply.

During the years from 1922 to 1929 the money supply in the United States was basically stable and so was the general price level. In the 1930's the United States went through a depression and the money and credit supply in the United States was 32 Billion Dollars.

In the year 1933 the money and credit supply dropped to 23.3 Billion Dollars this was a drop in the money and credit supply of 29%. The consumer Price Index in 1929 was 51.3 % figured (1967=100) was 51.3%. In 1933 the Consumer Price Index was down to 38.8 this was a decline of 24.4% in the general price level.

When one uses the general exchange equation first put forward by Irving Fisher in 1911 to show the relationship between price changes to changes in the money supply, we find that it is the average transactional money supply that we must use in the formula.

In 1929, the figure for money and credit is the average for that year. It is still basically the same as it had been for the year 1922. But the prices had been steadily declining from 1929 to 1933. The 1933 money and credit figures represent the figures for year end and not the average for 1933. When the average is computed it is less of a drop than when compared to the end of 1933 figures.

The actual drop in price between 1929 and 1933 is almost exactly identical to the decline in the general price level between those two years. Thus for some four hundred years up to the year of 1933 all facts fully substantiate the quantity of money price theory.

What evidence then do modern economists have to completely abandon the quality of money theory of prices in favor of the Keynesian Price Theory?

We also have the evidence that in every hyperinflation situation in history the general price level has moved in direct proportion to the changes in the money supply.

In 1935 John Maynard Keynes came out with his price theory which completely contradicts the then prevailing price theory.

The question we would ask modern economists today is what evidence do you have to completely abandon the quantity of money theory of prices in favor of the Keynesian Price Theory?

The research shows that since 1933 the money and credit supply in 1933 to 1943 when we finally returned to full employment that the money and credit supply had increased from 23.3 Billion dollars to 84.5 billion dollars which is an increase of 262.7%. While the consumer price index increased from 38.8 to 51.8 for an increase of 33.5%.

The change in the price was only about 13% of the change in the money supply. They would say doesn't this clearly show absorption of the money supply in production rather than price level change.

However they are ignoring the abnormal level of reserves the banks carried during the recovery years.

This was included in the money supply figures but was not circulating. This money is non-transactional money and does not enter into the exchange equation or have any bearing on the general price level change.

The removal of those reserve figures and using the true average figures looks more like the quantity theory or money rather than Keynesian price theory.

They would then counter that since the money and credit supply in 1933 was 23.3 billion dollars while in 1973 it was 450.5 billion dollars for an increase of 1833.5% while the consumer price index went from 38.8 in 1933 to 133.1 in 1973 for an increase of 243% and since reserves were normal for comparing these years that surely this clearly shows absorption.

This clearly shows that the money and credit supply is 7.5 times greater the increase in the money supply. The change in price shows only to be about 13% of the change in the growth of the money supply.

I have discovered that this is clearly not the case, I discovered this purely by accident between 1971 and 1973 which is not so. It was this discovery that led me into an intensive study of economics over the last seventeen years. These next paragraphs will show an unscientific comparison of prices between 1946 and 1971.

The comparison led to some startling conclusions on my part discovering the correlation between wages versus prices between 1946 and 1971. This comparison led to some startling conclusions on my part about what happened to wages versus prices of my clients about similar circumstances.

I was convinced that real wages for any given job had drastically dropped in real value between 1946 and 1971.

I did quite extensive research between several economic books written in 1909 and price comparisons between the years 1910 and 1973. I found drastic declines in real wages. I had no idea that this discovery was totally contradictory to everything taught in modern economics.

I interviewed several of my clients about their thoughts on this subject. I was convinced that the value of wages for any given job, had drastically dropped in real value between the years of 1946-1971. During this time I ordered some old copies of catalogs from 1902, 1908, and 1909. I also reviewed economic books written in 1909.

I was convinced that real wages for any given job had drastically dropped in real value between from 1902, 1908, and 1909. I also picked up several sets of business and economic books written in 1909. I did quite extensive long-term price comparisons between 1910 and 1973. I again found the same kind of drastic declines in real wages etc. I had no idea that what I had discovered was totally contradictory to everything taught in modern accounting books.

One day I while at a client's office I relayed something to a young professor of what I had discovered. It was there that I met a young economics' professor who had just finished his studies in economics and he stated that my research being totally different from the modern textbooks was totally wrong.

He brought his economic books and showed me where in all periods of inflation wages had lagged behind inflation that in post-depression year's wages had run ahead of inflation.

They claimed the increases in productivity and cost of living adjustments and strong labor unions etc. were responsible for this. The young professor showed me where I had said prices in 1971 were five times what they were in 1946 (on my part I was being conservative here I actually had measured seven to eight times).

The consumer price index change (58.5 in 1946 to 121.3 in 1971) indicated that 1971 prices were only 2,073 times 1946 prices.

If my dad needed to make 12,000 in 1971 to be the same as 2400 in 1946 he only needed to make $4975.20 to have the same earnings. Since he made $6400.00 in 1971 he was actually earning 29% more in 1971 than he did in 1946 rather than only 53.3% as much would be the case if the real price change had been what I had originally figured.

My measurement for price changes between 1910 and 1973 indicated that 1973 prices were 22.5 times higher than 1910 prices. Thus the average laborer who earned $500.00 in 1910 was earning the equivalent of $11,250.00 of 1973 money.

This was almost double what someone on minimum wage working sixty hours a week with time and a half for overtime would earn in 1973. Starting engineers salaries in 1910 were $3000.00 which would equate to a starting salary in 1973 dollars of $67,500.00.

But the actual starting salaries for engineers in 1973 was only about $12000 to $13000. The figures seem to show my measurements were way off.

The consumer price index in 1973 showed 133.1 while in 1910 it showed 31. According to the figures in the consumer price index the 1973 prices were only 4.29 times higher than the 1910 prices.

The 1910 prices were rather 22.5 times higher as I had measured, but if the consumer price index is right then the day laborer was only earning the equivalent of $ 2145.00 in 1973 money.

The person making minimum wage would approximately make about $6700. The starting engineer of 1910 would be making the equivalent of $12,870 in 1973 prices about the same as engineers were making in 1973.

The difference in the figures were indeed not close together at all would the measurement of price level changes between these two periods equal out. If the price index was correct, then my measurements were wrong.

My measurements showed that there was 6.5 real change between the 1910 and 1973 prices than the consumer price index, could the consumer price index me wrong by that much.

We needed to look a little bit further into the consumer price index, according to my research it was first called the cost of living index. The cost of living index was first set up in approximately 1947. According to a 1948 economic book the base was figured originally using the average prices from 1935 to 1939 for the base of 100.

The book has a listing of price relationships from 1913 to March of 1947. The interesting fact that if you have any one of these year's consumer price index on the 1967 base you can then convert the entire list into the 1967 base and find that every year exactly agrees with what the consumer price index indicates for these years in the 1967 base in any economic book.

This indicates that the consumer price index on the 1967 base is simply a restatement of the base from the original measurements. Those original measurements were long-term measurements and are highly accurate relative to each other.

Since from 1910 to 1946 prices never changed by more than 100% and we had periods of inflation then deflation then stable prices then deflation and then again inflation there is simply no room for error in measurement from 1910 to 1946.

However, since 1946 we have had steady inflation, in addition the measurements for 1946 forward are short term measurements which are inherently more likely to be in error than long-term measurements.

Both of my measurements 1946 to 1971 and 1910 to 1973 showed about the same error and for the same period of time-post 1946 years. It should be obvious that no one has ever measured any of the years 1910 to 1946 against the base year 1967. If such a measurement was done they would have immediately known that something very drastic had happened to the consumer price index measurements.

In taking those two long-term price comparisons, I had inadvertently done something that no economist would normally do and which no one working on the consumer price index had researched either. Therefore in my research I discovered something no one else was aware of that there was a drastic error in the consumer price index for the post 1946 years. I should also bring up that there is the same degree of error in the GNP deflator index.

I am a skilled carpenter and cabinet builder, if you told me that a twenty one and a half foot board was really three and a third feet long you might get by with it so long as I never saw the board.

Forty inches might come from the floor up to my waist but a twenty-one and a half foot board would be more than three times my height.

I am a certified public accountant skilled in number crunching and mathematics you could never lay out two sets of data before me whose averages differed by 2150% and have me confuse it with data whose averages differed by 329%.

The ones who put out the consumer price index could never be confused, the only way this error could occur is that no one looked at the data from those old years versus the 1967 base on any kind of long-term basis.

It is mathematically impossible for the price change between 1910 and 1971 to be only 329% increase. There are no cluster of price changes at or near that level, there are no prices that went up less than or went down in price but there are extremely large numbers of prices that went up extremely higher than that.

The laws of mathematics and averaging absolutely preclude any possibility that the price level changed for that period can be anywhere near what the consumer price index indicates.

The very nature of general price level increase's is such that any item whose real value has not changed much must have a price change that is essentially the same as the change in the general price level change.

Since between 1910 and 1973 prices those clusters are between 20 and 25 times the 1910 prices and the mid-point of that range—22.5 is the most likely price change.

One should be able to take any fairly stable commodity which has not had any great supply and demand change to effect prices and find that the change in that item would be essentially the same as the change in the general price level.

A good commodity for the 1910 to 1973 period would be the sixteen penny nails. In the 1908 Sears and Roebuck catalog you could buy 100 pounds of sixteen penny nails for $2.20. In 1973 the same amount would cost $50.00. Therefore these nail cost had increased 22.7272 times what they cost in the 1910 period.

If these nail had gone up only by what the consumer price indicated so that they would cost 4.29 times 1910 prices they would have cost only $9.45. What supply and demand factors could have possibly caused nails to go up in the price 6.6 times more than the change in the general price level.

The truth of the matter is no factor caused the nails to increase in price we can produce nails just as efficiently in 1973 as in 1910. If we had compared the same item when the consumer price index relationship was correct we would get a totally different picture.

We will take the same item the nails price from 1908 with a price from the Wards catalogue in 1922. If the nails had gone up strictly if the nails had gone up according to the consumer price index indicates the change in the price would cost $3.56 per 100 pounds in 1922.

They actually cost $3.03 per 100 pounds. This is exactly what you would expect as we could produce nails cheaper in 1922 than in 1910.

One might ask how much nails would cost in 1973 if the quantity of money theory of prices had been the correct theory of prices rather than the Keynesian theory of prices. We can use the consumer price index which is correct in its relationships as long as you stay pre 1946 to tell us the price change from 1910 to 1929 (where I have the money & credit figures).

In 1929 the consumer's price index shows 51.3, in 1910 it shows 31 making the 1929 prices 1.6548387 times the 1910 prices while the money and credit amounts for 1973 was 450.5 billion dollars while in 1929 it was 32.8 billion dollars. If the quantity theory of money held, it would make 1973 prices 13.73475 times higher than the 1929 prices. Multiplying 13.73475 by 1.6548387 we get how more 1973 prices should be than 1910 prices under the quantity of money theory of prices.

This yields a 1973 price 22.7288 times higher than 1910 prices which yields a price just .0016 different from what the actual change in the price of nails was at 22.7272 times the 1910 price. Is this just coincidence?

No I believe that it is not a coincidence. The consumer price index for post 1946 years is really and truly drastically in error and that error is a gross understatement. Real inflation has greatly exceeded what the consumer price index states.

Real wages have not gotten ahead of inflation, but they have fallen drastically behind. No cost adjustments based on the consumer price index have been anywhere near enough to adjust the real impact of inflation.

The impact of inflation on bookkeeping and taxes etc. has been much greater than anyone ever imagined.

Obviously, if the prices and money supply changed in direct proportioned to each other between 1910 and 1973 at least over the long-run then no long-term Keynesian type absorption of money supply changes into production changes could have occurred. The Keynesian price pattern simply did not happen.

We have further proof that the Keynesian pattern didn't occur. The Phillips curve shows that the inflation in post-World War II years has been higher than it was supposed to be based on Keynesian economics and that is based on comparing the price changes per the consumer price index which is grossly understated.

The Phillips Curve shows that inflation in post-World War II years has been higher than it was supposed to be based upon Keynesian economics and that is based upon comparing prices with the consumer price index which again is greatly understated.

The Phillips curve analysis economists now believe that there is a tradeoff between inflation and employment. The question in my mind is (Did they totally ignore the fact of between the years of 1922 and 1929 we had full employment in spite of population growth while having absolutely stable prices.)

They say that there are circumstances in which we can use the Keynesian spending solution without there being a tradeoff between inflation and full employment.

Apparently they mean conditions where we have high unemployment and low production such as during the 1930's depression. Economists routinely assume that this was the case during the recovery from the depression.

They assume that we did in fact increase spending calling forth more aggregate supply without much change in price during the recovery from the depression. They assume that the Keynesian price graph really happened during those years. Economists regularly say as much in their books while putting forth tables of information for the period which absolutely believes their assumptions and statements.

If the standard Keynesian price pattern had occurred during the recovery from the 1930's depression, here is what one should find when full employment returned in 1943. We should have come out of the depression at or near the 1933 price level.

Instead we find that rather than coming out at or near the consumer price index level of 38.8 (1933's CPI) we instead see the CPI at 51.8. This was practically identical to the 1922-1929 level of 51.3.

This is odd when price's dropped 24.4% unemployment became 24.9% and to increase employment back to full employment prices increased the same amount that employment increased.

In reference to the Keynesian economics theory is that nothing like this ever happens. There should be no correlation between employment and price level change. During the years of 1929 and

1943 there is almost a perfect one for one relationship between the change in price and the change in employment.

The trade-off between inflation and employment during the recovery years of the depression is nearly one for one. One of the effects of having a wrong consumer price index, wrong GNP deflator index is that all efforts to arrive at real changes in economic data is data are distorted from reality by the erroneous indexes.

The GNP (Gross National Product) for 1929 103.1 Billion dollars while in 1973 it was 1,289.1 Billion dollars. In order to compare these figures in real terms they must be converted to common year dollars. If 1973 prices were 4.29 times higher than 1929 as the consumer price indicates, we could multiply the 1929 GNP by 4.29 to put in it 1973 prices.

The 1929 Gross National Product (GNP) be 442.3 billion dollars in 1973 dollars. This would make the 1973 (GNP) 2.91 than the real (GNP) for 1929. If 1973 prices were 13.73 times higher 1929 prices as proven above, the situation is quite different.

The 1929 Gross National Product (GNP) in 1973 prices becomes 1,415.56 Billion dollars in 1973 dollars. The real (GNP) actually being 1.098 times the 1973 (GNP).

The real (GNP) declined further because of the population increase, it is hard for us to believe that we produced less in 1973 that we did in 1929 a large part of this could be in reference to President Nixon responsible for taking us off the gold standard in approximately 1970 -1971.

The

Keynesian

Economic

Theory

The Kensington Application to Economics is to insert money into the economy in a time of slow growth and increased unemployment claims. The money implemented into the economy will make up for the lack of sales or consumers using caution and saving more than spending. Introducing Stimulus drags our economy down not a surplus.

The New World Order is nothing new, nothing orderly, it is shadow government and will not bring prosperity. It has been tried before and failed. It is being tried again and it fails each time.

Franklin D Roosevelt
with emphasis

The Error

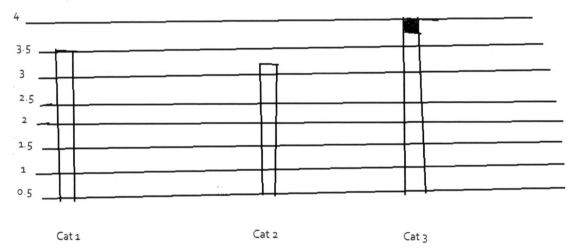

Cat 1   Cat 2   Cat 3

The Error shows a society out of control, the greed of those who believe in redistribution, a generation who demand priviledges but are not will to work for them. Our founding fathers legacy dying out to those who believe society owes them. We must return to basics.

The Error gives a glimpse at the debt our grandchildren will be expected to pay in taxes. The dreams of our founding fathers for this nation seeming to be dying out with our current level of greed.

The Redistribution of money promoting spending rather

Than saving central idea behind Keynesian economics

Influencing consumer behavior at micro-level.

Economics is the study of production, distribution, consumption of goods and services in the economy. John Maynard Keynes an economist lived between the years of 1883-1946 known best for his simple explanation of the cause of the Great Depression.

Keynes believed that the flow of money being the principal cause for the depression.

In October 29, 1929 there was a stock market crash this economic theory that by inducing stimulus into an economy that is in recession or depression there is a continual flow of money. The spending increases the earnings increase which increases more earnings.

In Keynes theory one person's spending goes to help another person's earning. He believes that during the Great Depression there were great numbers of people hoarding money keeping the economy at a standstill.

Keynes observed that modern economics differ from primitive or central planned economics. Keynes recommends that during high unemployment, recession to use the stabilization curve. This would give the people less freedom more regulation and the government more control over the people.

Adam Smith

Adam Smith introduced the laissez fare economic system, many economists say this system is used within the United States today. A free enterprise system with little government control. The problem with this system is when the people do not participate in government, the government establishes more control until the people have no liberty. The Soviet Union is an example of an economy where there is tight control over the people's creativity in recent years there may have been some improvement.

Where there is a lack of liberty there is loss of productivity as we see in the examination of economies where the base is not freedom but socialism. When people are able to be productive, creative the economy grows and there not only is a positive feeling in the nation but the surplus is up.

When people are threatened with over-taxation, productivity is stifled and growth is hindered. Our founding fathers found this to be true, and were determined to establish a government that would be best for all people. When government seeks to control every element of the peoples' there is a feeling of enslavement.

Therefore a big federal government is not the answer, the solution lies in taking responsibility for ourselves and our families The best solution is to serve God with all your heart, take care of your family and produce with creativity and liberty. A man who helps others through the way he lives his life is the example our founding fathers chose to give us for our legacy.

The change we ask for is not the change we received. We need to turn to the Lord Jesus Christ and ask him for help, He is our only hope today.

There are many seeking security, in many things, smoking, beer, material assets but all these lead to false peace. There are many searching but Our Lord and Savior said that He was the only way to be saved. He sinned not once, it is through him that there is eternal life.

Notes

The Error

They say that there are circumstances in which we can use the Keynesian spending solution without there being a tradeoff between inflation and full employment.

Apparently they mean conditions where we have high unemployment low production such as during the 1930's depression.

Economists routinely assume that this was the case during the recovery calling from the depression. They assume that what we did in fact increase spending calling forth more aggregate supply without much change in price during the recovery from the depression.

They assume the Keynesian price graph really happened during those years. Economists regularly say as much in their books while putting forth tables of information for the period which absolutely believes their assumptions and statements.

If standard Keynesian price pattern had occurred during the recovery from the 1930's depression, here is what one should find. Starting from the low point of the depression in 1933 and looking for when full employment returned in 1943. One should see essentially stable prices till we got near 1943. We should have come out of the depression at or near the 1933 price level.

But we find that rather than coming out at or near a consumer price index level of 38.8 the 1933's CPI we instead came out at 51.8 which is practically identical to the 1922-1929 level of 51.3.

It is odd that when prices dropped by 24.4% unemployment became 24.9% and to increase employment to full employment prices went up the same amount that employment increased.

Keynesian economics says this should not have happened. Keynesian economics says there should be no correlation between employment and price level changes. But between 1929 and 1943 there is almost a perfect one for one relationship between the change in price and the change in employment.

There was a tradeoff between inflation and employment during the recovery years of the depression but that tradeoff is nearly one for one. One of the effects of having a wrong consumer price index and wrong GNP deflator index is that all efforts to arrive at real changes in economic data are distorted from reality by the erroneous indexes.

The Gross National Product for 1929 was 103.1 Billion dollars while in 1973 it was 1,289.1 Billion dollars.

In order to compare these figures in real terms one must convert them to common year dollars.

If 1973 prices were 4.29 times higher than 1929 as the consumer price index indicates we could multiply the 1929 GNP by 4.29 to put it in 1973 prices. This would make the 1929 GNP to be 442.3 billion dollars in 1973 dollars.

This would make the 1929 GNP 2.91 times greater than the real GNP for 1929. But if 1973 prices were really 13.73 times higher than 1929 prices as we have stated above the situation is quite different.

The 1929 GNP in 1973 prices becomes $1,415.56 billion dollars in 1973 dollars. The 1929 real GNP was actually 1.098 times the 1973 GNP. The capital real GNP had declined even further because of the population increase. It is hard for us to believe that we produced less in 1973 than we did in 1929 this is really the case.

This data as stated was done many years ago, with inflation as it is now, the prices doubled comparative with the prices in 1973 We can see that by manufacturing our own products we would be better off keeping the jobs in America and not becoming a debtor nation. It is time to return to the steps of our forefathers.

Why General Price level tend to Equal Money Supply Changes.

There is a mechanism that I call the budget constraint mechanism which causes the general price level changes to end up being equal to the changes in the money supply. Everyone who has ever been or a fixed budget knows that for a given amount of money from period to period that any changes in spending cause a corresponding change in the previous spending habits.

If you are going to buy something that you have not bought before you must give up spending for something you previously bought because you have only the same amount of money you had previously.

If you decide to buy more of one item than previously then you must cut back on something else that you normally buy.

In economics, it is well known that when demand increases for any item and we try to buy more of that item it always results in an increase in that item's price which tends to call forth more production of that item.

It is also well known that when demand decreases for any items and we buy less of it the price will decline to try to sell the item and clear the market and this calls forth less production of that item.

In an economy that has a stable amount of money any attempt to buy more of one thing results necessarily in our buying less of something else.

The price on the item for which the there is more demand will go up, but the price on the item for which the demand declined will go down. The price increases and decreases will offset each other and there will be no change in the general price level.

If the economy has new money created and put into circulation, we can then buy new items without giving up any of our previous spending. The new items we buy have an increased demand and therefore the price goes up on them, but since nothing was forgone and suffered a demand decline and a price decline to offset the price increase on the items with increased demand the general price level will increase.

When new money is spent by anyone in the economy on an item whose price has not been adjusted it again acts as a new demand increasing the price. However there was no decline in purchasing of other items to cause a matching decline in price.

This process will continue the general price level change occurs throughout the economy in an amount exactly equal to the change in the money supply.

The same thing occurs in reverse when the money supply decreases. It acts as a decline in aggregate demand decreasing prices but with no matching or offsetting increases in prices. The changing in the money supply overtime always adjusts the general price level equally.

There can be short-term adjustments that are different but in the long run the changes in Money Supply and General Price level end up matching.

The Keynesian Price Theory wrongly felt that there could be a long-term actual absorption of money supply changes into production rather than changes in the price level but unfortunately it is not accurate.

Effects of Error in Price Theory on Keynesian Theory in General.

Let us try to understand why the general Keynesian theory can only work if the Keynesian price pattern exists we must look at the general exchange equation put forward by Irving Fisher back in 1911. This formula is based around the fact that aggregate spending is equal to aggregate selling. This formula means that everything sold must of necessity; also having been bought.

Mr. Fisher expressed this relationship in terms of Money, the number of transactions and the general price level. In the formula $M=$ the average money supply used to carry out the transactions.

V= the velocity or turnover of the total average money supply in carrying out the purchases during a given period of time. T= the number of transactions occurring during the period expressed in equivalent $1.00 transactions.

P= the unit price being $1.00, bought in the base year thus P= the General Price Level.

When comparing two years one year is the base where the unit price is $1.00 and the other year uses a price P that is the equivalent in real value to what $1.00 bought in the base year. This being we substantiate that P is the General Price Level.

The equation says that M times V equals T times P. The money supply times the velocity or turnover equals total spending. The number of transactions times their unit price equals the total level of selling. There is absolutely no doubt about the fact that this is the correct formula for exchange through a monetary system.

In almost every economic book this formula is mentioned most of the economic books give you a discussion that is fair.

I have questions about these discussions and find many of them shallow and incomplete and in most instances wrong.

In studying various economic books I have found that most will show the fact that you can solve for each of the variables in terms of the other three.

In general they give you a vague idea of how the formula is interrupted to give the quantity of money theory of prices and somehow it is interpreted to arrive at the Keynesian price theory.

Nearly all books give me the idea that there is no practical way to understanding the actual workings of the formula and the reaction to particular changes to particular items.

There are three major weaknesses to every analysis of this equation that I see having reviewed hundreds of economic books. First the equation can be written as an equations of two different ratios and then two other equations of the inverse of those ratios.

I have never seen an economic book that ever showed the equation as an equation of ratios. The ratio of the money supply to the number of transactions is equal to the velocity of money to the price level.

The ratio of the money supply to the price level is equal to the ratio of the velocity of money to the number of transactions. These two ratios and their inverses are always equal at all times.

If we take the ratio of $M/P = V/T$ and under the circumstances where M=P we are looking at the quantity of money theory of prices. When the change in the money supply is equal to change in price then the change in velocity must also equal the change in price then the change in velocity must also change in the number of transactions.

In this case, it is the change in the transactions which is the cause and it is the change in the velocity of money which accommodates the change in T (supply side of economics).

If we take the equation of ratios where $M/T = V/P$ under the circumstances where M=T and therefore V=P and with the special provision that the change in V and P = zero we would be looking at the Keynesian Price theory.

The change in M or money supply acting as a change in aggregate demand called forth an equivalent change in real transactions T leaving velocity to equal the change in the price level.

Since the increased production supposedly could be bought for the same price the price change would be zero and therefore so would the change in velocity would be zero. Much can be learned from examination of the ratios that show that certain changes are related to other changes in other items.

The second problem in traditional examination of this formula is that economists want to put the total money supply including both the transactional and non-transactional cash into the variable M in the exchange equation.

This is theoretically incorrect.

The equation is the exchange equation and it should only contain the average money supply that was spend on the items bought (P times T)

The non-transactional cash has a zero velocity because it was not spent on P times T. If you are trying to put non-transactional money into the formula one must decrease V (velocity) to accommodate the change in M since the non-transactional money is then transferred to transactional money and had no effect on P or T.

It is treated not as change in the money supply, (because they have already included in the money supply.) But rather as a change in velocity of the money supply.

In doing this they confuse an item which is really a change in M in terms of transactional money supply with a change in velocity.

In most of my research I find they added approximately sixteen or so factors to be associated with the velocity which really have nothing to do with velocity or its real meaning.

This also distorts the real meanings of the ratios as well. In developing an overall theory one does not need to throw all the money into the exchange equation.

I would keep the exchange equation separate from non-transactional cash then deal with the movements of cash from non-transactional to transactional and vice versa as separate items. Then you don't throw in confusion into the analysis of the most important and fundamental of all economic equations.

The third problem I see is the economists do not make proper analysis as to which items in the equation are essentially independent input variables and thus causative variables and which variables are essentially not independent input variables and thus effectively only effects of the changes in the independent input variables.

Money obviously is the most independent input variable in the entire system. It seems that we can pretty well make the money supply whatever we want it to be.

The only other element in the equation that can move around with money is the general price level.

The general price level is not an independent input variable the general price level is an effect not a cause. The only causative item that can match the freedom of movement of the general price level is the money supply.

Therefore the chief cause of changes in the general price level, is the change of the money supply. Velocity for all practical purposes is not an independent input variable.

The main reason that economics have wrongly treated it as an independent input variable is because they threw non-transactional money into the variable M and therefore treated items which were really changes in transactional M as being changes in V.

I believe the right use of only transactional money in M eliminates all of those items which really changes in M being attributed to V leaving V and non-independent input variable.

Velocity is essentially an effect and not a cause. T, however is both cause and effect. It is possible to have a change caused by a change in M but it can also change quite independent of any of the other variables in the equation.

Changes in technology, capital, and other items can cause T to change regardless of changes in any of the other variables.

Velocity of the money supply then changes to accommodate the changes in T that were not caused by a change in the money supply.

There are certain things that are not ascertained about this equation that you do not find in economic books.

Since M is transactional cash, you cannot add to M without adding an equal amount to P times T. Money has to be spent on P times T in order to get into M. The change in P times T caused by a change in M, when it is first spent has to be equal to the change in M.

This is also equally true when M is reduced, or not spent-moved to non-transactional cash. In this instance P times T must be reduced by the same amount as M.

It is very easy to think that one of the major effects of changes in the money supply is to substitute money supply for velocity.

One could spend two dollars twice to buy four dollars' worth of goods or one could spend four dollars to buy four dollars' worth of goods.

Why couldn't you just add two dollars to buy two dollars' worth of goods and use the existing two dollars only once to buy two dollars?

When a change in M occurs it must be spent P times T. Since the change in P times T is the same as the change in M and since the change in velocity is equal to the change in (P times T) divided by M a change in M never originally causes a change in velocity.

This is because the change in P times T caused by a change in M is equal to the change in M. Velocity might slow down later, but it is never the original effect of a change in M to cause a change in velocity.

A change in the money supply can therefore cause only three possible things.

1. A change in transactions directly proportional to the change in M with no change in the general price level.

2. A change in the price level equal to a change in the money supply with no change in the transactions.

3. Some change in transactions and some change in price such that the product of the changes yields a change in P times T that is equal to the change in M.

The change in the money supply can only act as a change in transactions to the extent that it does not cause a change in the general price level and it can only cause a change in the general price level to the extent that it does not change transactions.

This leads us to the discussion of real money versus nominal money. The M our equation is known as nominal money.

If we divide M by P we get real money. In any one turnover of the money supply M how many real transactions T will be purchased depends on the general price level or unit value of money

It is not the change in M, that determines how much change in T will take place but it is the change in M divided by P or real money change that determines what change in real transactions T will take place in one turnover of the money.

Therefore if a change in M takes place while prices remain stable that change in M will cause an exactly matching change in real transactions T. This is precisely what Keynesian economics claims will happen as long as we are at a point below the inelasticity of supply.

However if the change in M is matched by a change in P then the change in M can cause no change in real transactions T at all. This means that when we are concerned with a change in the money supply acting as a changed in the aggregate demand we are concerned with the change in the real money rather than nominal money.

A real change in real aggregate demand calls forth a real change in aggregate supply. But real aggregate supply is not P times T but just T.

Real aggregate supply T=MV/P. Therefore for a change in M to ever represent to any degree a change in aggregate demand it must be only to the extent that the change in M differs from the from the change in P or the general price level.

Keynesians would claim that the depression occurred due to the decline in aggregate demand that came from the approximately twenty five percent decline in the money and credit supply which was matched by an approximate 25% unemployment rate and an approximate 28% drop in real production (GNP).

But since the decline in the money and credit supply between 1929 and 1933 was almost exactly identical to the change in the general price level, the real money supply did not change.

Since the real money supply (M/P) did not change, the 1933 the money and credit would buy just as much real transactions in one turnover of the money M of 1929 would in one turnover.

Therefore one must ask why did the real production drop matched by a corresponding drop in employment and accommodated by a matching drop in velocity occur.

This is the $64,000 dollar question that no economist of economic theory has yet to explain. It might further be asked that if during the recovery period we really also might further be asked that if during the recovery period we really also had a price change that basically matched the real change in the transactional money supply.

Therefore the change in M again could not represent or act as an increase in aggregate demand in coming out of the depression, why did the economy recover and employment return to full employment by 1943?

The Keynesian claim that we increased the level of spending (aggregate demand) calling forth more aggregate supply but this is not the case.

The matching change in P precluded from being the mechanism. Keynesian economics is entirely based around the concept of changing the level of spending (aggregate demand) basically by changing the money supply.

But in order for this to work the general price level must not change to equal the change in the money supply because if it does it completely nullifies the change in the money supply from acting as a change in aggregate demand.

Keynesian economics has only one answer for unemployment or low production. The answer is always an increase in the level of spending which is an increase in the money supply.

Unfortunately this means further inflation or devaluation of the real purchasing power of the dollar. It also means larger government, deficit spending, huge government debts, distortion of the tax laws, and huge trade deficit caused by the difference in value of the dollar in the international exchange.

Today many places have stop accepting the dollar, requiring travelers to pay in their currency. The United States is the only nation that doesn't have to pay their debts to other nations in foreign money. This allows the government to print money as it deems necessary further devaluing the dollar.

Did you know that every time money is printed they have to present collateral? The collateral is every property's owners land, meaning they put you up for sale. This also means further inflation or deflation of the real purchasing power of the dollar.

In addition this means a larger government bigger deficit spending huge government debts, distortion of the tax laws and a huge trade deficit cause by the difference in the value between the domestic dollar and the value of the dollar in international exchange.

The more stimulus that the federal government passes the bigger the deficit our grandchildren are being required to pay, the burden we pass on to our children is not a legacy it is a shame.

The further the dollar goes down the less it is worth then this will cause us to have purchase more of another nation's money to pay our bills because of our financial picture. The IMF has the authority to change the reserve currencies.

Every corporation has to balance their books at the end of the year, so should the federal government be called into accountability but not to be passed on to our children and grandchildren. We are not passing a legacy on to our children we are passing a yoke of bondage in this writer's view.

We are known as the biggest debtor nation, we have corporations that outsource because or taxes are out of control.

These corporations receive tax breaks, and are able to make ends meet, paying lower taxes, and paying lower wages. The tags on our clothes say Made in U.S.A but some come from India, China. Our representatives should work for us, represent us, a few do, but many do not represent us they work for their own self interests.

This is because we have forgotten that we the American People have a voice and we are being too complacent. The idea that complacency leads to apathy is very real today. We need to stand up for our basic rights and freedoms before they go away.

Distortion

A

New Economic

Theory to Explain

The Depression!

I believe that the changes in the money supply going into the depression caused the depression not by directly acting as changes in the aggregate demand but by changing the general price level. It was a mechanism related to the changes in the general price level which caused the drop in production and employment. The same thing and the same mechanism were responsible for the changes coming out of the depression.

Economists have recognized that the price level changes can act as redistributive forces in the economy and that they can be distorting factors on various items, but they have never recognized any ability of general price level changes to directly or indirectly change the real level of production and employment in the economy.

I am not saying that general price level changes are direct causes of changes in production and employment. I am not saying that general price level changes are direct independent input variables in the general exchange equation they are not.

I am saying that the general exchange question is recursive. This means that something which is purely an effect can by certain means end up effecting one of the independent input variables into the equation even though the item itself is not an independent input variable.

I believe that general price level changes effect changes in production, not directly, but indirectly. There are important differences between direct and indirect effects.

The direct action of independent input variable into the general exchange equation is always the same. But the indirect effects upon the general input variables are always different.

Sometimes a general price level change will cause one effect, but under different circumstances it cause the opposite effect and under some circumstances it will cause no effect at all. Thus the rise in general price level is not necessarily the same in effect as another rise under different circumstances. One price decrease is not the same as another price decrease.

One period of stable prices is not the same in effect as another period of stable prices. In 1921 we had 17.5% deflation in one year the immediate short-term effect was to increase unemployment to about 10%.

It is usually listed as a depression, however the price decline was actually good for the economy. The economy immediately rebounded to full employment and stayed there for seven years. This was done without any increase in the money supply and the price level also remained absolutely stable for seven years between the years of 1922-1929.

Production per man hour continuously increased throughout this period etc. The price decline between 1929 and 1933 of some 25% was not good for the economy at all. There was no movement to rebound from the depression at all.

If prices hadn't risen back to the 1929 level we would have remained in a state of depression. Only restoration of the lost price level could ease us out of the depression of the 1930's.

If we had stabilized prices at the1933 level we would not have had a boom such as we had between 1922 and 1929 but rather we would have stayed at the 25% unemployment level.

Let us diverge to discuss another system which works basically the same way relative to the general price level-namely the historical cost basis accounting system. Everyone knows that the accounting system is based on historical cost basis without adjustment for price level changes becomes distorted and inaccurate due to general price level changes.

This is due to the fact that many items such as old inventory costs, depreciable assets, and debt retirements are recorded at historical costs based on the value of the dollar at the time the original transaction occurred and are now compared with current items in a quite different value of the dollar.

But on the books the two quite different dollars are treated as though they were the same. Thus this shows even though the accounting theory is accurate the difference in the dollar value causes the books to be inaccurate. We can take a look for a moment at what happened to the general accuracy of the accounting system over the period of 1910 through 1933.

If we compare the prices between the years of 1910 and 1920 we will find that the prices have approximately doubled. The average prices of the fixed items in the economy was rising as new items came on at higher price but not as much as the current price level had risen.

It must be kept in mind that it is the fixed items which become distorted. The overall distortion that occurs is basically close to what the difference is between the current price level and what the average price level of the fixed items in the economy cost. In 1920 the general price level had doubled, but the average price of fixed items had only risen about 62%.

In 1921 due to revaluation etc. prices dropped till the current price level was also only about 62% above the 1910 prices.

Toward the end of 1920 the CPI (Consumer Price Index) was 60.14 compared to approximately 31 for 1910, but by 1922 it had declined to 50.08 which was 1.62 times 1910 prices.

If one were to continue to use the historical cost basis of accounting prices had been adjusted as close to the average price of the historical cost fixed items as possible and thus the distortion error in the bookkeeping system had been minimized.

It would seem that the bookkeeping system had been more accurate in 1922 than in 1920. The price decline took out distortion that had been previously introduced by the price increase between the 1910 and 1920.

There then followed a period of seven years of prosperity and high capital addition that occurred at the approximately the same price that existed in 1922. Thus by 1929 the accounting system was essentially as accurate as it had ever been and distortion was at an all-time low. All long term debts, assets, and inventories were in the 1929 price in 1929.

The deflation of prices set in between 1929 and 1933 whereby prices declined approximately 24.4% this introduced a flat out across the board 24.4% distortion on every long time debt and long term asset in existence.

In 1933 new capital assets were being added at the new lower prices approximately only one sixteenth the cost in 1929. During the years 1929 to 1943 the price of the long-term fixed items hardly bobbled from the 1929 price but the current price levels were far below the 1929 level until 1943.

We can measure from 1929 to 1943 almost exactly how much distortion existed in any given year by taking the difference between the year's consumer price index and the consumer price index in 1929. In each case that would be the amount of average distortion of the bookkeeping system.

It should be noted that sales at breakeven being based on fixed assets distorted by exactly this same amount. It should be referenced if prices had been locked in or stabilized at the 1933 level that this would have locked in a 24.4% distortion rate until all the long-term distorted items worked themselves out of the economy which would have taken years.

The general price level rose coming out of the depression the distortion rate was decreasing until 1943 when we came out of the depression and returned to the 1929 price level. This was the point the distortion in the bookkeeping system had been basically eradicated and the books again became as accurate as it was possible for them to be based on historical cost.

There was an obvious difference between the price drop in 1921 which eliminated distortion and the price drop between the price drop between 1929 and 1933 which introduced distortion. There also is a difference between the stable prices at the 1922 level to 1929 because it was a the same price as the historical cost and what we would have had if the prices had stabilized at the 1933 level where the 24.4% distortion existed.

There is no doubt concerning the fact that if we were examining the accuracy of the accounting system from 1929 to 1943 we would find that the difference between each year's price level and the price level of 1929 would be an exact measurement of the distortion and therefore the measure of the inefficiency of the accounting system.

It should therefore stand to reason that the same distortion effect could possibly be a measure of the efficiency of the operation of the monetary system in its ability to carry on trade.

If this were the case and the efficiency of the monetary system could be a causative factor in controlling how much production for exchange could take place and be exchanged, then price distortion could become a direct cause of a change in the level of production and employment.

In our modern economy practically everything is produced for exchange by a monetary system. Sometimes we forget that we actually have two systems-the economic system and the monetary system.

We forget that the economic systems' efficiency cannot exceed the efficiency of the monetary system in carrying on the exchange that the production is produced for. It is a known fact in economics that more production can be had and at more efficiency if you can have production for exchange or trade rather than for personal consumption.

It is also a known fact that you can have more production for exchange under a monetary system that you can have under a pure barter system because the monetary system is a more efficient system of exchange than a pure barter system.

The question we should be asking is why should we have a reduction in trade directly caused by the inefficiency in the workings of the monetary system due to price level distortion coupled with the bookkeeping system with the system of debt repayment?

The question also arises why should we not be able to have an increase in production and employment caused by the removal of price level distortion from an economy? I believe it is possible to have these things?

Changes in the money supply end up changing the general price level. Changes in the General Price Level either introduce or remove price distortion into the economy. Price distortion directly and proportionately effects the efficiency of the monetary system as well as the bookkeeping and break even computations as well as tax laws.

This change in efficiency of the monetary system directly effects the general efficiency of the economy as a whole and thus can cause a drop in production and employment as distortion increases or an increase in production and employment as distortion decreases.

It should also be pointed out that distortion can be caused just as much by inflation and by deflation although it may five a false sense of progress and optimism which may partly offset the effects of the distortion.

Efficiency is an optimization process. Some certain combination of things give optimum or near optimum performance, but any departure from those circumstances decreases efficiency regardless of which direction the movement is in.

If we grant that price distortion could potentially be a causative factor in changing the level of production, it then remains to look at the Depression and the recovery from the depression to see if price distortion is related to the change in the level of production and employment.

We can do this quite easily for the time period 1929 to 1943. I have already reviewed the movement of historical cost data above so that it should be recognized that each year's consumer price index as a percent of the 1929 price is the efficiency rate.

We can either compare this efficiency rate with the rate of employment or we can take the difference between each year's consumer price index and that of 1929 and compare it with the unemployment rate.

The unemployment rate does not account for all the unemployed many that are not able to file, those who decide not to file, and those who decide it is not worth the effort. The employment rate as a percent is a very good measure of the relative efficiency rate of the economy.

What we are comparing here is the efficiency of the monetary system as measured by the degree of distortion or non-distortion introduced by price changes with how efficiently the economy operated based on how efficiently it employed the workforce.

When we compare each year's consumer price index with the 1929 index as a percent then compare it with the employment percent each year from 1929 to 1943 we find that they are indeed related to each and every year to at least a 94% relationship and most of the time the relationship is nearly 100%.

When one averages the correlation ratios for the entire fifteen years the relationship come out to 99.4% correlation. If we ignored frictional unemployment in 1929 to 1943 it would almost be a perfect 100% correlation.

Price Distortion is the only potentially causative item which correlates almost perfectly with the amount of unemployment for every single year of the depression or recovery from the depression.

It is almost absolutely certain that this is the cause of the depression and our recovery from it.

The fabrication of markets, currencies the instability of the stock market establishes currencies that are over-valuated. These are the days where the banking system seeks to establish inflated accounting system. This is the perception of the consumer, loss of hope in their future their country and their leaders. Turn back to God, He is our only hope, He is our salvation.

I believe we are approaching a time in history to come, when we like Israel are disobedient to God. We like Israel were indulgent in every whim of evil to be found and we will be punished.

The Almighty God punished Israel by letting a foreign ruler not only overtake her as a nation but transport her brightest and best of her land out of Israel into a foreign land to serve as prisoners.

We are approaching such a time when we cannot control our borders and we have a wave of immigrants coming in as never before seen.

We will have a harsh and evil ruler to govern this land and the sins of the people will be evident. This ruler will destroy all that is good and prosperous in the land.

We as a nation have sinned and we must repent, and make correct choices. We must live as we are supposed to as Proverbs dictate. We must realize that God owns this land and it cannot be sold to another nation.

When this nation turns from God, and lets little children be persecuted by the public schools, and we have done this today. When we take prayer out of schools, and take Bibles away from children and put in jail those who pray to God before taking a test. We are in the wrong.

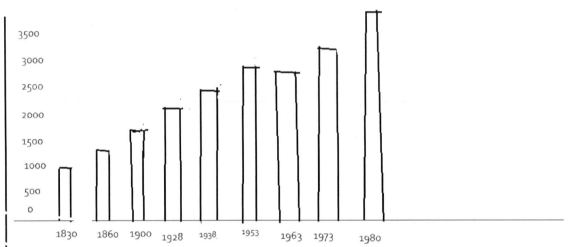

The more factories, the increase in products made in America. The higher the GNP, the more countries depended on us instead of today where we are dependent on them. The automobile industry, the steel industry, only one nation could come close to America and that was Germany. The steel industry, where we set the grade of the steel to build ships, to build railroads that was of standard quality and pride was ours that stated made in America. We are a great nation, but we trusted oil, money and our greed for gold is our sin, we must remember that no nation flaunts sin before God and gets away with it.

Obviously the Federal Reserve coupled with the people's panic runs on the banks which caused the drop in the money and credit supply which caused the decline in price which in turn introduced price distortion which was the real culprit in creating the 1930's depression.

Increases in the money supply put back into circulation for whatever reason or by whatever means had the effect of increasing prices which removed the price distortion and allowed the economy to resume full employment by 1943 when we return to the same price level as 1929. This was also the same level as the average price of all long-term fixed items in the economy.

To measure distortion and its effects for the depression years is extremely easy, but to measure distortion and its effects for post-depression years is extremely difficult. We have had better than forty years of continuous inflation with fixed items coming into existence and better than forty different prices. It takes far more energy, information and resources than I have at my disposal to make a study of distortion effects in the post-depression years.

I am however, firmly convinced that Keynesian economic policy did not get us out of depression by means of the supposed mechanism of changing aggregate demand and it has not really and cannot really be the answer to our current economic problems either. Distortion is still the main culprit involved in practically every economic woe we have.

Distortion management is what the government policy should really be and it surely wouldn't call for forty years of continuous inflation at fairly high levels.

It also doesn't call big, interventionist government, deficit spending, high taxation income redistribution and welfarism. These are all the legacy of Keynesian economics and socialism.

Let me point out something about distortion that we need to understand. We must understand the difference between the inflation rate and the distortion rate. When you first start having inflation, the distortion rate and the inflation rate are the same.

Later however, the rate of distortion is cumulative and compounding. If prices have increased till what used to cost $1.00 now costs $20.00 then five percent inflation will add another $1.00 to the cost.

The five percent inflation becomes a 100% distortion rate addition. It must be recognized that the real distortion rate at this point is actually two thousand percent and it will remain at two thousand percent if you stabilize prices and have no further inflation.

This means that a three of four percent inflation rate does not mean the same thing that the same rate meant back in the 1940's or 1950's. It also means that if we stopped having inflation now, it would not mean that distortion or its effects will automatically or quickly disappear from the economy. Those distortion effects will remain for years.

The research for this document done many years ago still points to where we are today with trillions in the hole, stimulus that does not work, consumption of oil more than we can produce.

The oil must peak at some point and then the wheels will stop, where will our fast consuming economy be then, we must conserve and use our resources wisely.

The silence from the noise of the trains, the wheels of the trucks that deliver our commodities to the store. If we do not have truck drivers to drive the trucks how will be receive those products.

In my opinion greed always has a price, the protests for fifteen dollars an hour for minimum wage entry level work has a price. The closure of many family owned business's because they cannot afford to pay that price. The elimination of the small business owner is in the plans for those who seek destruction of this nation.

We have not been wise stewards taking care of what we were given by our Heavenly Father. We waste ten times more than we conserve, we pollute and have sense of ingratitude and a desire for greed. We need to realize there is a price for our sins and there is a redeemer who died for us, do we disregard the heavy price he paid.

Why the Keynesian

Theory

Is Wrong!

The Keynesian Theory being tried by President Roosevelt, President Ford, and many others to include President Obama the theory does not work, it is a manner of questionable ethics to try the same process over and over and achieving the same results.

The New World Order is nothing new because it was also tried during the depression the only thing accomplished is money being moved around but not being increased.

The Stimulus is only a temporary fix, bonds must be repaid, rebates only work temporarily the debt falls upon our children and grandchildren we must not leave them such a legacy.

The Keynesian Theory believes that by introducing additional stimulus, results in more dollars being spent raising the GDP helping the economy helping both the worker and the unemployed at the same time.

There are a few diehards who still believe that the stimulus is responsible for the economy still operating today.

The Keynesian Economics being tried in 1920's, 1930's and the effects of the Obama Administration politics referencing the bailouts of various business giving the government more control in private affairs have not helped the economy instead we have a bigger debt that perhaps any generation before us to pass on to our children to pay off.

The hedge funds desiring to take control of the real estate market, the stock market, the derivatives, the subsidies the banks playing the currencies to incur more profit for themselves. The introduction of new currencies like the bit-coin and many others arriving on the market.

The desire of many involved in real estate to inflate prices as to hedge their losses. A homeowner buying a whole block of houses just so he will not have neighbors. The accelerated real estate prices $989,000 for one house. The rents of $3,458.00 per month in the New York and California districts. These statistics put the ability of the public to be subservient to the rich and greedy.

Outsourcing has taken a whole new level in the technology age, the ability of scam artists to resolve blame to the robot's in order to keep gains obtain illegally. They blame the robot and take no responsibility for themselves.

The contracts go to the highest bidder in one estimation, but to keep cost low most of our products assembled in a foreign country. The Chinese seek an alternative from the dollar as the basis of the world's financial system a threat to China's economy.

The United States a nation founded on the belief one nation under God, needs to return to the concept of the founding fathers of this nation put in place seeking God's wisdom. We have storms, fires, famines over every part of this nation that God Almighty established.

Many economists forecast an event we call a bank holiday, which is an event that exceeds beyond normal expectations in the areas of banking, finance and to some extent the unemployment statistics'.

Money allows us to exchange goods and services, invest in specialties, start corporations, build a legacy for our youth and facilitate an economic advantage.

Credit in an economy

Individual taxpayers must balance a checkbook every month, the federal government must realize that there is a payday in our very near future. During the time this book is being published there are nations deciding how to devalue the dollar because of the United States reckless spending habits.

The

Appian

Way

The Appian Ways being one of the roads that led to Rome, today we live in a modern Rome with all roads leading to deceit and corruption. In Rome under Nero the Christians were to blame for the fire, the burning of Rome. But Nero desired a scapegoat someone to blame because he desired a different type of Rome.

Under Nero the Christians were portrayed as sheep and sacrificed in the arena. Today they are lined up dressed in orange and shot, beheaded or abused many other ways.

This is where we are, but let us turn our focus upon to where we were and examine the trail of our errors. The road to enlightenment is often painful but we may learn many things along the way.

Let us turn our attention to 1939, Germany desire to be master of Europe collapsing, Japan's race for the Far East in trouble, Churchill was in trouble in Britain. The international order had arrived the old system disappearing the new order arising. The United States, and the USSR as superpowers and the United States the victor.

In the years 1940 to 1944 the industrial expansion of production grew rapidly and the out of physical goods grew beyond our greatest expectations. The United States growth rate approximately 20% a year majority due to war production.

During this time in history, when majority of the world's powers were suffering the United States became richer. The manufacturing our own products and providing them to the world took place in the United States.

This is a contrast between a nation who manufactured products and now buys products from other nations. A contrast between an exporter and an importer. This is a nation blessed by God and now a nation enslaved by her sins because of her choices.

During the years 1939 to 1943 Washington possessed gold reserves of 20 Billion just thirteen billion less that the world's total of 33 Billion. The United States in these years became known as the world's greatest shipbuilder. This was largely due to massive growth from manufacturing expansion during the war. It owned approximate one third of the world supply of shipbuilding facilities.

The below chart shows that Europe's share of the manufacturing was lower than at any time since the start of the eighteenth century. Today our share of the manufacturing output is lower than it has been since at least the 1940's.

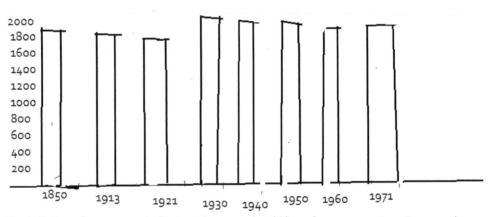

1850 - 1971

1970-1971 President Richard Nixion
took the United States off the Gold Standard

The inflation of 1971 - 1973 indicates where we should have been as a nation. Our morals declined as our prosperity increased. Our values turned to Gold, Oil instead of God.

The Loss of Innocence

The Loss of Innocence for the United States started in the 1970's when President Nixon took the United States off the Gold Standard. The subject of economic power is important to every nation because the economic power of a nation determines its future. President Nixon stated that "economic power" will be the key to other kinds of power", which can be seen today in the shape of the world's politics'.

The subject of closed societies or shadow governments have existed all the way as far as the Bavarian empire and many influences before them. A closed society operates behind the scenes using various figures to make the changes in governments they desire.

The lack of published figures to measure the income and the product, the bouncing exchange rates possibly leading to President Nixon abandoning the gold exchange rate and excepting exchange rates that never stayed the same. The gold standard an acceptable and reliable standard abandoned for exchange rates that are flexible with no chance for stability. The businessman succeeds leaving the general public with no stability.

The next chart shows after the Second World War approximately between the years of 1954 to 1977 a remarkable growth rate. The production of manufacturing industries the change to industrialization this is to say the difference between our glorious past to our present status.

The increase in production by manufactured goods, recovery of war torn economies the slope from agricultural to industry and the coming of age of the third world countries.

In 1957 manufactured goods out-produced agricultural goods this also included Minerals this was due to the continued drift from farming to planned economies. Today we see a drift to robotics and service economies which will not show the production of the industrialization age.

Too Far Too Fast

The title of this chapter will start to bring us to where we are today in financial, economics and the falling gold prices in the years 1958-1962. We observed that in the United States increased production faster than any other country, mass production, and mass consumption and declining in values.

The values of high consumption, mass production also involved low personal savings. The desire for flashy cars, color television sets, expanding military budgets. The increase in military spending during the Kennedy, Johnson administrations to include Vietnam War.

The 1960's to 1970's problems began to arise industrial un-competitiveness, government deficits turning toward a financial vehicle known as Eurodollars. The United States share of the world's gold reserves shrank tremendously from 68% to 27%. These occurrences led President Nixon to take the United States off the gold standard and float the dollar against other currencies.

The high inflation experienced in the United States in the 1970's causing the dollar to weaken against the Japan, France, Germany currencies, oil stocks which incurred addition complications. The decreasing productivity from the 1970's to 1980's due to failure to maintain production to compete with their foreign rivals.

The American GNP once the highest in the world, began to fall, perhaps we were not good stewards of what the Almighty God had blessed us with and perhaps we still are not good stewards of what we still have today.

We helped the many nations recover after the war, in the years of 1939 to 1945 approximately; in return they granted us military courtesies like setting up a base in their country. We were mass producing, and enjoying the fruits of our labor but no one realized the party had a heavy price tag many years down the road.

Today in the 21st Century 18 Trillion dollars in debt we have become a debtor nation instead a nation which lends to other countries and helps them in their time of need. We have immigration problems of which we cannot control. These immigration ordeals now have cost us more than we can deal with today. We have drugs coming into the country by the Mexican Cartel and other nationalities. This is the reason we need security at our borders, the same situation exists in Germany, Italy, France with millions foreign immigrants in Germany alone.

We are known to the world as Modern Rome, a country founded on the belief in the one true Almighty God who created world from nothing, man creates with materials, and God does not! We have stretched ourselves beyond our supply lands, we have allowed other gods into our land. We have allowed our kindergarten children to be corrupted with a form of evolution at the tender age of four and five.

The idea is to indoctrinate them early, the mind is a sponge absorbing what we read, hear, watch on television are taught in schools. The enemy knows that the younger they start public school the less foundation working parents will have time to instill in them core values of the Bible. The more susceptible they will be to the ideas of indoctrination.

We seem to be interested in turning out robots, those who just take orders without being able to think for themselves. This is a problem when a sixteen year old boy cannot do third grade math, the multiplication tables nor pass a simple comprehension test that equals out to a fifth grade level when given a diagnostic test.

We need more Christian Schools, I see many cities building more schools and staffing them with teachers. We need Christian educators, teachers more than we need additional government schools to handle the overflow.

We have forgotten the God of Abraham, Isaac and Jacob and the Ten Commandments the basics upon which our nation was founded upon. We must return to Almighty God for our nation to heal the many wounds that it has open. We must put our hope in the one who can help Jesus Christ.

The Bible tells us when a nation, society has too much, we become full of ourselves self-indulgence, pride, greed and the lust for more. We are satisfied with nothing, and we imagine our own gods, and sometimes we incur vanity making self a god.

We are advancing to fast much like General Rommel under Adolf Hitler he advanced to far above his supply lines and both he and his soldiers suffered. We are trying to be a policemen to the world, and sometimes the world laughs at us not with us!

Israel is correct on many issues, she does not advocate open borders, being in the Middle East she is faced with many enemies and many people want to eat off of her surplus. Israel knows she must limit the amount of foreigners into her land, her neighbors will become too hungry. It is a well-known proverb, "a hungry man does not ask he just takes".

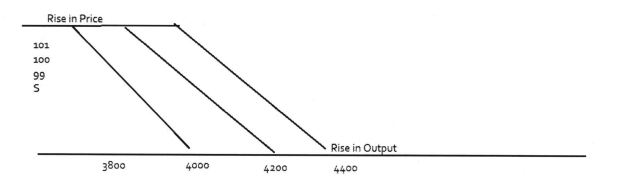

Billions of Dollars

Rise in Price

101
100
99
S

Rise in Output

3800   4000   4200   4400

Israel in Crisis

The Israeli election won by Prime Minister Netanyahu sparked some animosity in this nation's administration. There is less support for Israel in the United States in comparison to previous years. Israel is our ally and we owe her devotion and allegiance. This means standing with her in front of the United Nations in my opinion.

Every day is a challenge in Israel from getting on the bus to being a soldier in the (IDF) Israel Defense Forces. The IDF received a report that they suspected one or more terrorist organizations interested in poisoning water in swimming pools and local water in Israel.

They suspected the major route the terrorist would use would be a tunnel near the Gaza Strip. These tunnels are often found in Israel, this is the major way of moving drugs, hostages, and ammunitions from different parts of Palestine into Israel.

This tunnel was elaborate, electrical outlets were found, many other modern conveniences were found like a railroad car to move ammunition's between towns. This tunnel said to be about 120 meters long extended beneath the Israeli controlled border fence and road which splits between the town of Rallagh.

I recommend Victor Mordecai's "Christian Revival for Israel Survival" it is a book well worth reading in which many facts that we do not know about events that have taken place since before the twin towers tragedy shed considerable insight.

A store in Bethlehem supplied a semi-automatic rifle and three pistols by the owner of this store. While the interrogation of a well-known terror suspect with ties to Osama Bin Laden revealed a rather large shipment from Iran arrived in Israel via the Dead Sea.

The Jerusalem Post, wrote the article originating in London. The Moslem activist known as an imam reportedly to have links to Saudi born dissident Osama Bin Landen was arrested yesterday. The imam in question is well connected and has many supporters through Shari Law organizations. It is believed that Saudi born dissident Osama Bin Laden published a seventeen page death threat prior to the attack on the twin towers. This document targeted the United States and other enemies of Islam.

The group representing Muslims in Great Britain were quick to advocate that the imam who has a distinguishing metal law had committed no crime. They were representing demands for his release upon his status as a representative of promoting Shari Law. The imam in question whose stepson and son were arrested late last year in Yemen on possible charges with plotting bombs and a hostage taking plot.

This two articles give us just a little taste of what Israel deals with on a daily basis. The names have been omitted to protect sources, organizations and legalities. We should all urge our leaders to support Israel instead of instituting sanctions. We should support Israel instead of using tools like the United Nations to force Israel to give more concessions to Hamas and other terrorist agencies.

We must consider Prime Minister B. Netanyahu warning to the Congress, that we basically do not want to make this kind of a treaty with an enemy of Israel.

Iran has sworn to annihilate Israel, and this piece of information is interesting considering the agreements our nation is considering with Iran. In my opinion Iran will use the United States to do the following, make a nuclear weapon, and continue their efforts to bring attacks against Israel using their neighbors like Syria.

The establishment of a Palestine Statehood considered an important step by some in the European Union. Doing so the leaders said would be in the best interest of Israel. The declaration of the EU to state that the Palestinians have a right to Jerusalem as their capital on its national soil.

The Palestinians envy Israel, they make much lower salaries than that of Jews & Christians counterparts. In my opinion, the Palestinians have more children and desire the affluent land of Israel but they only want to live off the dough but not at the expense of an Israeli Sovereign State.

The more land that Israel withdraws from and gives to them, the more land the PA will insist belongs to them. The citizens of Israel have given up to much, some of their citizens have had to vacate and live without a home because of the Palestinians'.

A possible note here is that these dates reflect a period from approximately 1992- 2005. All dates are approximation.

The bombings of the Jewish synagogues do not become less frequent, the attacks of Christians on Easter have not become less and less. The EU under resolution 181 request Israel to return to the borders of 1948.

This being advocated by PLO Observer Nasser Kidwa in letter to Secretary General Kofi Annan. These reports are from the year

March 28, 1998-1999, it is my opinion that the PA does not want peace with Israel it wants to do away with Israel. I believe Israel should stand and not give any more land to the PA. I believe when we negotiate with terrorist they will never be satisfied.

The writings of Victor Mordecai, well recommended by this author, to awaken us to the truth of the happenings in the world around us.

The

Change

Of

A

Nation

The change of a nation, from reliance upon God Almighty to the respect for none. The change from abstaining from evil to embracing iniquity. The change of obedience to apathy and then to indifference. The change of teaching the Word of God in the home to division in families. The change of forgiving one another to endorsing hate and refusing to forgive one another.

The change of making our own products to being one of the biggest debtor nations there is today. When we put God first, teaching our children to obey God with reverence we put the family as an asset instead of a demerit.

The change of leaders being bought by other countries, being the servants of greed. We need leaders that will do the right thing, establish policies because it is the right thing to do. We do not need leaders that will bow to the opposition when it is against God's law. If we put sin before God then we will incur the wrath of God.

I do not recognize this nation anymore, one the founding father's established America to be a beacon a light to show the world the right path. The more secular we become the more like Europe we become, I am not sure at this point if we are able to tell the difference.

America a nation established to be light to dispel the darkness, now has been corrupted into the realm of darkness. I ask the question what will it take for America to wake up and see where her choices have led her.

The change from independence to an indebted welfare state, with many young students declining to attend college. The lack of ambition, the lack of diligence the increase of moral decay we need change today to return to the ways of the founding fathers.

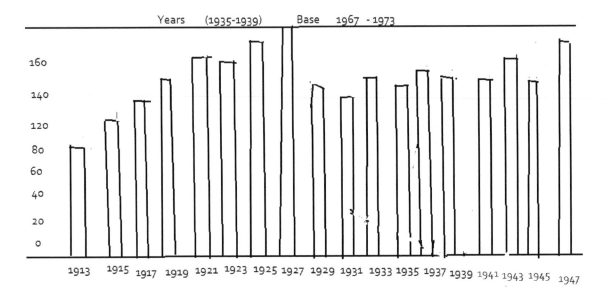

This graph helps illustrate America as a nation, whose purpose to be a beacon to others, in these graphs she has not forgotten her God!

The Founding Father's

The founding fathers of the United States of America sought for the freedom of religion, freedom to own their own weapons. The freedom for their children to be taught the word of God, to be taught how to read, write and arithmetic. These are the basic freedoms our founding fathers fought for when the nation was in its infancy.

Our founding fathers wrote the Declaration of Independence upon the common knowledge of government social order and morality based upon the Bible, which is the word of God.

The founding fathers valued human life, everyone's life is a gift from God, in Exodus 20:13 Thou shalt not kill, this is a commandment from God. In Matthew 22:39 Thou shalt love thy neighbor as thyself. My belief in this commandment tells us we are our brother's keeper, the love of our country should be greater than the love of self.

If the world as a whole does not respect life to i.e. the born as well as the unborn all other moral values that a nation possesses are without value.

In the beginning God created man, and from man, he created woman a helpmate for man, thus forming a union between man and wife. The core of society is the family unit, the children are seeds to carry on the values of the family unit. The children are to grow in nurture and admiration of the Almighty God, the God of Abraham, Isaac, and Jacob.

When man has corrupted what God has put together, a nation begins to fall away from the core values and become just people living in the same household. If you take a look around at the morals of society today you will see the first step on the road to ruin is demoralization of the family unit.

Our founding fathers pioneered this nation with a diligent hand, America's freedom did not come easy, and it came with great sacrifice. The cold winter of the soldiers, in Valley Forge, some without socks and shoes still preserved on in spite of hardships. The colonists believed in a nation founded on the principle "one nation under God".

The Bible states in 2 Thessalonians 3:10 "For even when we were with you, this we commanded you that if any would not work neither should he eat." The colonist believed to improve yourself as you learn, meaning learn as you go, and prosper as you learn. In those days men and women possessed an honest day's work ethic, they did not want anything handed to them they sought to earn their wages.

Our first president George Washington believed in Proverbs 1:7 "The fear of the Lord is the beginning of knowledge, but fools despise wisdom and instruction". The beginning concept of life is to know God who created the earth, and his Son Jesus Christ without Jesus no man will see God.

The founding fathers sought for their children to grow up with a foundation centered on God. The textbook "The New England Primer" many of the principles came straight from the Bible.

When taught the A, B, C's each letter related to a concept of God i.e. A –In Adam's fall we learn all have sinned. The letter B relates to a Biblically mind. The letter C relates let me be more considerate of thee. The Letter D relates to let me be more diligent in my studies.

The Abrahamic Covenant states that if a person or nation obeys God observing his commandments, that person or nation will be blessed. Our founding fathers believed that in producing God-fearing children, teaching them fear of the Lord that they would be blessed. In Proverbs 14:34 the Bible tells us that "Righteousness exalts a nation but sin is a reproach to any people."

We as a nation have been blessed because of our support of Israel and of Israel's support of us. We have a covenant with the Almighty God the Creator of this world. We also have a covenant with Israel, we owe this nation much and we have been blessed in the past because of our support of her today.

In Matthew 22:39 The Bible tells us to love thy neighbor as thyself. America has done this helping restore war torn nations, sending humanitarian aid to other nations food, clothing, grain, missionaries to teach other nations how to grow food.

We are personally accountable to God to know that one day we will stand before God to give an account of how we used his resources. We will give account for our actions, our decision, our thoughts, our motives, our sins and our crimes against one another. In

Hebrews 9:27 "And it is appointed unto men once to die but after this the judgement."

We now live in one of the darkest times in history, a nation founded upon God, forsaking God, abandoning His principles and commandments. A nation inviting other gods into a land dedicated to "One nation under God". The question we must ask ourselves is did not Israel do this and this nation is the apple of God's eye.

The freedom to worship, the freedom of religion, and the freedom of speech is becoming more restricted every day by our government. The Internet now being overtaken by the government, the Healthcare Law now becoming a right, not a privilege.

We as a Christian Nation are to be the "light of the world". We must realize that in addition to putting God first in our lives, that we must also take a stand for God in the event that our leaders have forgotten to put God first in their decisions.

We are in the mess we are in today because we as a Christian nation have not stood up against those who do not advocate Godly Moral Values today. Our nation today needs repentance, not just being sorrow for our sin but turning from our sin. God loves the sinner but hates the sin.

In James 4:17 "To him that knoweth to do good and doeth it not to him it is a sin". When fighting for truth and justice in a land where sin is a way of life we must remember George Washington's example to preserve although he did not win every battle he won the war, not by his might but by his faith in Almighty God.

In Luke 9:62 Our Lord taught us once we put our hands to the plow never to look back, we will persevere. Abraham Lincoln believed in the Almighty God, and I believe he was thankful for all that he had, and all that he was blessed with.

While we live in the land of the free and we are thankful for calling America our home. We must not forget of those who sacrificed much so that we their descendants could enjoy the privileges that we take so for granted.

Our founding fathers were willing to lay down their lives rather than remain slaves or become servants to tyranny. Patrick Henry once stated "Is life so dear or sweet as to be purchased at the chains of slavery?" Forbid it Almighty God! I know not what course others take but as for me give me liberty or give me death!

The question I put out to all Americans is "How many of you could honestly say that today?" We as a Christian Nation have grown too complacent, we have grown in apathy. We care not for the welfare of our fellow man. We have grown too accustomed to sitting in front of the television and have become coach potatoes.

This is why our youth, many of them sit back and rely on the government to send them a handout. It is true that there are some who are disabled and cannot work. But many rely on the government to make their living for them.

This is where our young have become involved in sin, a temporary pleasure that has far reaching consequences. We must learn what we sow we will reap, idleness is the devil's workshop, honest wages never hurt anyone.

We must learn to trust God, and not ourselves whereby human wisdom is no wisdom at all it is folly. But many chose folly as a way of life and indulge in sin and all the trappings. The choices will have far reaching consequences' to defer as far as the destruction of their own family.

This is where our society is going as we become more a secular nation, adopting the policies of Europe. We as a conservative nation used to lead the world, now we are being led by the world into bad economic policies.

The stimulus we the American people did not want in total, now is coming back to haunt us. The principle of redistribution of wealth, builds anger between those who have and those who are in poverty. The give me concept is adherent many of the twenty year old's generation today. They do not have the work-ethic of their parents and are resentful of the substance of their parents.

We are a society incurred with more taxes placed upon us than any before, this is why our founding fathers came to America for a better life. We are taxed before we see our paycheck, then there are those who want to tax us again on what we spend. I believe there is a day coming when we must "Stand." We must defend the Word of God, with prayer and supplication and with our life. Prayer as one of my dear friends used to always remind me "changes things".

Let us as a nation forsake our greed and our pride and turn back to the Almighty God who is the only one that can heal our land. He rules the nations, He can set a wicked ruler on the throne or he can set a righteous one. Let us ask God what we can do to turn our country back to him. Let us ask God what we can do to turn our schools from government schools back to Godly Schools, in which our kids learn the ABC's instead of prejudice.

The destruction of a nation starts from within, small wars started within the very unit that established the nation. The family, if the family unit can be destroyed you have brother against brother, sister against sister, mother against father until divorce is not the exception but has become commonplace norm.

The concept of a divided nation is that it cannot stand together one of our founding fathers stated that if we do not stand together we will each fall separately. The idea of establishing a crisis state where politicians can be bought by other nations to influence the policy's that want to see established in this nation is a type of shadow government.

The shadow government seeks to establish problems where none exist. One example would be in the mode of electronic warfare to use false intelligence against two countries that do not like each other pulling both nations into war. This is one example of how wars are started to accomplish an objective for the government that is not in the war money i.e. greed.

Lawrence Ashley's Appeal

The Need for Help to Get These Ideas
before Economists and to the Public.

If you are at all familiar with economics, as I believe you are, you will recognize that nobody else is saying anything close to what I have said in this book. This is all new and totally different material from anything presented anywhere by anyone. This is one hundred percent my own analysis and discoveries and thinking. It is totally original.

I have spent time off and on for seventeen years studying and analyzing economic data and reading economic books.

Approximately all economic books are written by liberals or socialists which is a strange situation for a free enterprise-capitalist nation. I believe what is put forward in these books is just plain wrong and without foundation.

I have several concerns about my studies through the years. First, they won't do any good if they aren't made public knowledge. Our country and indeed the world is in a horrible shape because we haven't had this knowledge and unfortunately it isn't getting any better.

These studies by Lawrence Ashley can be used to help others economists and politicians today. It is an eye opening study for anyone to show where we were where we are going and what we need to do to change our course. The sum of all things is involved in choices, will we make the right ones, the hard decisions necessary to get our nation back on the right track and off the road to enslavement.

Lawrence Ashley is gone on to glory, at the date of this writing. Lawrence was a brilliant man and suffered many years from dialysis and possible kidney failure for the last nine years of his life.

These ideas will benefit many corporations, and influence the way we think of our world today. This is a tribute to a brilliant man who simply wanted to make a difference in the world by his contribution.

I simply want Lawrence's ideas to benefit others.

Esther O'Gallagher

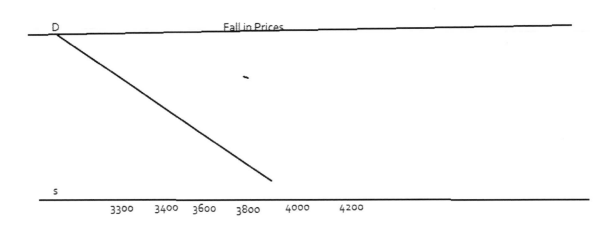

Expassionary Policy

D   Fall in Prices

S

        3300   3400   3600   3800   4000   4200

Expassionary Policy

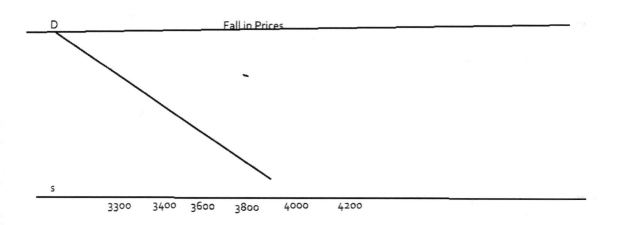

Fall in Prices

D

S

3300   3400   3600   3800   4000   4200

Per Capital
Relating To the Powers in 1950

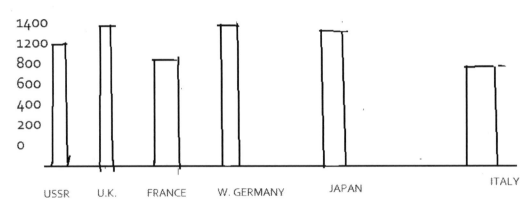

USSR	U.K.	FRANCE	W. GERMANY	JAPAN	ITALY

UNITED STATES   381 Billion
USSR   126 Billion
U.K. GREAT BRITIAN 71 Billion
France   51 Billion
Japan   35 Billion   Italy   25 Billion

The numbers above given in approximation indicate where we were, when we trusted God. The depravity of our nation, brings us to dependence on another.

Notes

Notes